T0198866

YOU DIRTY ROTTEN FILTHY PIG

Middle-aged Women Do Not Yell at the Men in their Lives

Allyson Moore

Order this book online at www.trafford.com
or email orders@trafford.com

Most Trafford titles are also available at major online book retailers.

Printed in the United States of America.

ISBN: 978-1-4669-4980-5 (sc)
ISBN: 978-1-4669-4979-9 (e)

Trafford rev. 07/25/2012

 www.trafford.com

North America & international
toll-free: 1 888 232 4444 (USA & Canada)
phone: 250 383 6864 ♦ fax: 812 355 4082

CONTENTS

Curse 1

It Sucks 2

Sitting 3

Sex Kills 5

Charlatan 6

Toe Nails 7

Currents 8

Temptation 9

Jump 10

Dirty Boy 11

Hell 13

The Drunk 14

Concubine 15

Losing You 17

Reflections 18

Mildew 19

Silently Standing 20

Fart 21

Indifferent Embrace 22

Baxter 23

I Can't Let Go 24

Not Goodbye 25

Bathroom 26

Jealous 27

Relationship Ended 28

Lost 29

Impending Presence 30

Why Would I? 31

Bum 32

What the Hell 33

Crumbs 34

Dreams 35

Corner 36

Chess 37

Boredom Day Friend 38

Stop Looking 40

The Silence of Your Love 41

Housekeeping 42

Carelessness 43

Poke In The Eye 44

In An Instant 45

Reason 46

I Wish 47

Weight 48

Without You 49

Expression 50

Not You 51

Lap Dance 52

Hurt...53

Not Forever Love..54

Wrapped Packages 55

Yet..56

Reclamation...58

Shattered 59

Diapers 60

Gone 61

Fool..62

Red Thong 63

New Chapter 64

Last Dance 65

Free...66

I Asked...68

Leaving 70

Past Time 71

Hole..72

Flavor of the Week 73

Stop 74

Preferably Alone 75

Thoughts While Writing a Report.........................76

Nouveau Trash..77

Tasteful Memories 78

Target..79

Cauterize 81

Bondage 82

Bobbit 83

No Choice 84

Significant Other 85

So There! 86

The Cassock 87

Belonging 89

Moving On 90

You Pig 91

Sunlight 92

It's Discouraging to Know 93

Toxic 94

Manners 95

Pining 96

Hump 97

Myth 98

Deception 99

Alone 100

Rent 101

Withdraw 102

Wedding Cake 103

It Is Hard To Let Go 104

No Justice 105

Connection 106

Farted 107

Landfill 108

Adoration 109

Birthday 110

Harm 111

Crap 112

Phone 113

Blame 114

Lessons 116

Drove 117

The Weekend 118

I Took It Away 119

Alone Again 120

The Female Zohan 121

Departure 122

Cast Off 123

Politics 124

Precipice 125

Hook Dick 126

Good Bye 127

Stench 128

Instant 129

Closing 130

CURSE

Drop dead
You dirty rotten filthy pig
As these words come out
I retract them

I want to scream
But stifle it
Good girls do not yell at lovers
No matter what they have done

How could you do this to me
You selfish
Heartless
Freak?

Irish Catholic middle-aged women
Do not throw things at men
I however would like to take a baseball bat to your
    head
And take my chances with going to hell

Allyson Moore

It Sucks

I can't yell at you
Although I would like to do so
Nice girls
Don't do that

I can't scream at you
Use four letter words
Let you know in no uncertain terms
How much you hurt me

Society dictates that I keep
My mouth shut
That I suffer in silence
While you get away with it

I guess I'm no Teresa

Sitting

Today I sat and
Waited for the email
That never came

A thousand times
I clicked
Send and receive

But there was nothing from you

Today I sat and
Waited in earnest
For you to call me

But your call never came

A hundred times
I jumped
When the phone rang

But it was only those stupid solicitation calls

Tonight
I sit in my loneliness
Despairing that I have not heard from you

Tomorrow
I will sit again
And wait

SEX KILLS

Oh
Oh
Oh baby
OMG
Baby
I'm going to explode
And indeed you did
Filling me with yourself

As you climbed off of me
You mentioned that sex had
Never before given you a headache
Twenty-four hours later
You were hospitalized
The force of our lovemaking
Precipitating a brain aneurism
That nearly killed you

CHARLATAN

Believing that I was street wise
I am surprised that
I got hooked
By you

I thought that I had more intelligence
Than to allow a man like you into my life
I did not know that I was susceptible
To a man who was such a whore

I thought my independence
Would keep me out of harms way
My path having been forged
Without dependency upon anyone

I thought that I could
Discern the charlatans
Perceive the deceivers
But clearly I was wrong

As a predator senses its
Victim's vulnerabilities
You preyed upon mine
Then attacked and conquered

TOE NAILS

Ugh!
You cut me again you Jack Ass
How many times do I have to ask you
To cut your toe nails?

Ouch!
I got sliced again
As we cuddled together while we slept
You woke me with your little toe razors

My ankles look like
Someone sliced me with blades
What would it take
For you to clip them?

Dumb Ass

CURRENTS

Docile though I appear to be
Nothing is further from the truth

Although my aspect is one of calmness
I am a cauldron inside

Tranquil waters
Bespeak great depths

Buried currents signify great strength
Masking my tortured emotions

Temptation

Temptation filled me
Then led me
To start to dial your number
Self preservation drove me
To disconnect the call

In my need to be loved
I nearly gave in
And sought it from one
From whom it is not capable
I will not make that mistake again

JUMP

Freedom escapes me
As I seek
To elude your grasp

I pretend not to listen
For the phone to ring
But I do

I am trained to fulfill your needs
In order that
Mine will be filled

The ringtone shrieks
I jump
Regret doing so

Yet bound
I am to you
Inexorably

Dirty Boy

How do you think I feel
Sitting here
Watching you
Act like you are normal

When I know the truth about you?

How do you think I feel
Hearing you
Talk like
A schoolboy in love

When I know how nasty you are?

How do you think I feel
Seeing you
Move on
To a new relationship

When I know that you run as soon as you feel
commitment coming on?

Allyson Moore

You are a dirty
Little boy
As you boasted
So arrogantly

With a filthy mouth
A racist tongue
You drink too much
Bathe too little

It is time for you to crawl back into that pig sty that
you call home!

HELL

Life with you
Would have been hell
On top of that
You do smell

When did you ever
Take a bath?
Or use a washcloth
To clean your hmmm . . . lap?

I've never seen you wash your face
Or put your clothes in their proper place
Your closet is the open floor
It's gotten so bad I can't see the carpet anymore

P is for puke
Which is how you make me feel
When I see the food on your stove
Which is congealed

Empty liquor bottles stacked against the door
There are so many there you could start a store
So much trash abounds
Guinness your cat cannot be found

Allyson Moore

THE DRUNK

Flushed brow
Uneven breath
Sweaty hands
You smell like death

Pustules of food
Interspersed throughout your beard
Droplets of drool
Scattered everywhere

Dirty shirt
Upon your back
Shitty stains
All over your slacks

Concubine

We were cuddling in bed
When your cell rang
You jumped up
Running across the room
Saying "It's a friend"

You told her that you were somewhere else
Though you were with me
When I asked you about it
You shrugged it off cavalierly
She told you that her mother died

She is no friend
Now neither am I
We are modern day concubines
Held in bondage
Slaves no less

Insufficient available men
To a growing number of women
Our emotional impoverishment
Leaves us vulnerable
To predatory males

Though I wish that it were
Otherwise
This is the last time
That I will share myself
With you

Losing You

Terror at losing you
Filled my thoughts
Distorted my perceptions

I sought to cling to you
Rather than to lose myself

In my desperation
Not to be alone
You seized my heart
Then squeezed my life out of it

Reflections

If I could change anything
I would have said that
I wished to change you

In seeking to change you
It was me who
Needed to be transformed

The image that I saw
Played back to me
Was the reflection of my own desperation

MILDEW

The mildew in the shower
Is beginning to become
Indicative of our relationship

What would it take for you
To spend a few moments
Scrubbing the walls?

Pristine whiteness
Has now given way to the
Growth of Petri dish like life forms

Allyson Moore

Silently Standing

Jennifer slipped quietly
Into the room
Seeking to soothe my sobs

She gently touched me
Stroked my shoulders
Kissed my forehead

Unobtrusive
She stood there
Sharing my pain

Witnessing my humiliation
Giving me strength
Reminding me that I was loved

FART

Far do'elle
Fart do well
Oh my goodness
Your farts do smell

Stink bombs detonating
In our bed
Toxic cloud
Hanging o'er our heads

Gaseous blips
Waking me from sleep
Do something to stop them
You fucking creep

INDIFFERENT EMBRACE

As you pull your car
Into my driveway
I try to see if you are excited to see me

As you move slowly
From your car into my arms
I try to assess your mood

Having not determined if I should give you
The control of knowing how much I missed you
I falter

Unable to resist
I naively rush
Into your indifferent embrace

BAXTER

I will take care of you
No one will ever hurt you again
I am not like other men
Trust me

Such were the lies
That you told me
I was an asshole
For believing them

Deceived I was by a man
Who is less than the
Person of my dog
Baxter

Allyson Moore

I Can't Let Go

C'mon you jerk
Our offices are only 10 feet apart
The least that you could do
After a nine month
Tempestuous
Office relationship
Is acknowledge
That I am still alive

You won't even look at me
Even though a month ago
You were begging me
To give you blow jobs in the basement
Expecting me to guard your secret
That after 6 pm
While you can't get your dick up
You always get a fifth of Grey Goose down

NOT GOODBYE

There is a part of me that wants to cry
To not let you go
Although I forced you to leave
I never wanted to say goodbye

Once given
My heart cannot be retracted
You will always be a lingering presence in my life
Albeit not in the destructive form that it is now

BATHROOM

Toilet seats have hinges
For a reason
So you can put them down

Bathrooms have toilet paper
In case you miss the bowl
And decorate the walls

There is a purpose for the racks
So you can use them
Instead of dropping towels on the floor

Sinks have faucets
So you can wash those hands that have been
"God knows where"

The bathroom has a can of freshener
So you can clear the air
Of your decay

JEALOUS

Jealous rage
Drove you to scream at me in the office
You lied when you said that you
Admired my intelligence

When I was promoted over you
You had meltdown
In that instant
We were done

RELATIONSHIP ENDED

My body rots
I long for the fresh air
Hot sun
Penetrating heat

These cold days
Dark nights
Eat at my soul
Claw at my heart

Your presence suffocates me
I am as though stripped
Needing release
Seeking peace

I patiently wait
For spring to come
That you may be gone
My spirit rebirthed

LOST

Gradually
I stopped sharing stories about you
With my girlfriends

They got sick and tired
Of hearing me cry
About the things that you did to me

They urged me to move on
When I could not
I was not ready to leave you

I became more isolated
Withdrawn from them
Eventually abandoned by you as well

Allyson Moore

IMPENDING PRESENCE

Your impending presence is like a cloak that
Tightens around my neck
And threatens to strangle me

Pull tight the cords
And my breathing
Becomes erratic

Puffs of cold air
Hang in the thick darkness
Choking me as I gasp for life

Why Would I?

Although I wish that it were otherwise
The reality is that I am still toxically joined with you

Unwittingly I gave you the power
To hurt me

With full knowledge
I now reclaim it

I release my heart from you
So that it is free to find its true soul mate

The chaos present when you are in my life
I dispel

My emotions which are in a frenzy when you are here
I calm

Knees shaking
I try to catch my breath

As I throw out every physical reminder
Of you

BUM

My father told me to
Stay away from n'er do wells
On top of that
You do smell

Plaque is encrusted
Upon your teeth
Mold spores are growing
On your feet

Bushy hair grows
Everywhere
Stains are on your
Underwear

Best I run
With all my might
Your absence of hygiene is
Quite a fright

WHAT THE HELL

You have a new love
In your life
Why waste your time on me?

You have given your heart
To someone else
Why waste her time on you?

What kind of game are you playing?
We crashed and burned
In flames in the office

You wasted no time in moving on
On hooking up within hours it seemed
Why the hell are you still contacting me?

CRUMBS

Beacons of hope are all I sought
Crumbs
Minuscule fragments of yourself

For those I would have been happy
So desperate
Was I to feel your love

In your carelessness
You could not even seek
To divulge yourself of those scraps

What a pig you are
Such a selfish bastard
Shame on you!

Dreams

There was a face
That I was hoping to see
In my dreams
It was you

I went to sleep anxiously
Hoping that you would come to me
But you did not
You had killed my dreams

Allyson Moore

CORNER

Pain unyielding
Unbending
How could you do this to me?

You said that you loved me
That I was "the one"
How could you lie to me?

You pig!
You swore that you would never hurt me
How could you treat me like this?

I gave my vagina to you
I allowed you to see into my soul
How could you have betrayed my trust?

In those moments when I turned the corner
And saw you kissing another woman
I felt like a knife went through my heart

CHESS

Innocent
Seeking love
And a bit of fun
Your seduction
Lead me to believe that you were something
That you were not

Players on a level playing field?
Not so
Pawn and prey
More like it
King takes Queen
Strips her of her dignity

Her tiara shattered
Her defenses destroyed
The game ends

Allyson Moore

Boredom Day Friend

I am your boredom day friend
The one that you talk with
When no one else is around

You sign on
In the hope that
Someone
Anyone
Will be there for you to chat with

Finding none
You go in search of mischief
Perusing Craigslist
The personals
Anything to capture your fleeting interest

I sense an inner smile
When you see
That I have logged on
Yippee
You have a playmate for a while

You Dirty Rotten Filthy Pig

The conversation goes well
Until I stop asking you questions about yourself
Then your attention begins to wane
Your interest was not in me
I am your boredom day friend

Stop Looking

Stop looking at me
If you do
Then I can stop
Looking at you

What kind of sick game
Are you playing?
You flirt with me as though
Nothing has changed

I broke up with you
Yet within 24 hours
You were out having sex
While I cried my heart out

Stop looking at me
Before I pour some ice
On that erection
In your pants

THE SILENCE OF YOUR LOVE

The silence of your love
Hurts me
Wounds me
In many ways

The silence of your words
Distracts me
Makes me
Want to run away

The lack of your presence
In my daily life
Makes me want to
Sob my life away

Allyson Moore

Housekeeping

Pick up your clothes
You dirty bum

Who taught you to be like that?
You filthy swine

The dishes go in the dishwasher
You lazy creep

Did your Mother really teach you that?
You stupid jerk

Put the food back in the refrigerator
You careless slob

Do you think that I have money to throw away?
You careless pig

This is not a slop house
Although you seem to intend it to be

Clean it up
Or leave

CARELESSNESS

How dare you be careless of my heart
I entrusted it to you
In your selfishness
You shattered it

How dare you tell me that you love me
Knowing that I would believe you
Then emotionally pull
Out of our relationship

How dare you spend our courtship staring into my
    eyes
Stroking my hand
Only to abandon me
Once your conquest of me had been achieved

The rawness of my emotions
Consumes me
I have been deceived by you
With only myself to blame

Allyson Moore

POKE IN THE EYE

I want to be loved
But you are not it
I'd rather be beaten
With a long wooden stick

A poke in the eye
A punch to the face
Would be better by far
Than be stuck in this place

You can hurt me all night
I can cry all day long
But truth be it told
I'm better off all alone

IN AN INSTANT

In an instant
I knew that you had lied again
Your eyes betrayed you
Your tone gave you away

In an instant
My internal antenna went up
I went into defensive mode
Knowing that I would have to protect myself

In an instant
It finally dawned on me what was going on
I was so disgusted
I wanted to throw up

In an instant
I knew who you were
I was overcome by the filth of you
Finally realizing
What you are

REASON

Challenges abounded
From them
I could not keep myself

As a pole seeks its opposite
For completion
I held on to you

Without demonstrable reason
I could not let go
Until you once again provided it

I Wish

I wish that I could reach out and touch you
I wish that I could turn my head and hear you speak
I wish that when my heart jumped at the thought of
    you
That I could gaze into your eyes

I wish that as the seasons passed
That I knew that I would be in your life
I wish that as my hair turned grayer
That you would be by my side as we slept at night

I wish that I could sing to you as you died
Embracing you
Instead of witnessing the carnage
This final affair inflicted upon our lives

Allyson Moore

WEIGHT

Every day of anger
Feels like I add another pound
Pringles and ice cream
Heal broken hearts

When am I going
To stop stuffing my face
Full of substitutes for you?
You are not worth it

One week later you are already
With another woman
While I come home with Reese's Peanut Butter Cups
To soothe my pain

WITHOUT YOU

You had a life without me
I could not expect you
To give it up
To join mine

Yet I did
At the moment of
That first deep
Intimate kiss

I had hoped that you
Would keep your love
For me
Alone

Only later discovering
That I was one of many
With whom you shared your body
But not your soul

If you will not give yourself
To me solely
You cannot have me
Find some other slut to be with

EXPRESSION

The eyes are the telling portal
The doorway to wisdom
They betray duplicity
Or confirm truth

Your hands upon my hips
Your ravaged kisses upon my breasts
Meant nothing
Unless we were joined at our hearts

I looked deep into the depths of your eyes
In shock I discovered the truth about you
Terror filling me that I had
Surrendered my heart and soul to you

NOT YOU

I don't want the last man that holds me in his arms
To be you

I don't want to read steamy romance novels
And only picture you

I don't want to be an old lady thinking about her last
     sex
And it was with you

I awoke in horror this morning
Realizing that I had given up my search

It may be you
Unless I change it

Allyson Moore

LAP DANCE

Tendrils of hair floated
Across my eyes
In a whimsical moment
You casually brushed them aside
Then gently nuzzled my lips

I felt eager to cast myself
Astride your lap
Ready to begin those motions
That would bring us both to climax
Then remembering the reasons why I will not

HURT

You don't care
Sitting in your chair
You are smug
Content with yourself

I am devastated
Sitting in my chair
I want to cry
Upset with myself for being so

Men and women
Are so different from one another
One lets go
The other does not

I wish that it were reversed
I would like to see you cry
While I sat there stoically
Watching as you lost control of yourself

Allyson Moore

Not Forever Love

Shawn
Said that he would love me forever
I believed him

When the signs came
That this was not true
I ignored them

I wanted to continue
The illusion that he loved me
That I was worthy of his love

How could he have ever
Deceived me
When he claimed to love me so deeply?

I just don't get it
Would someone please explain it to me?
I'm afraid that I will never get over this

WRAPPED PACKAGES

Dynamic charisma
Must be accompanied by humility
In order for followers
To have faith in the message of the leader

You are a wanton vessel
An empty carriage
A false prophet
You play a dangerous game

Waiting to be exposed
Removing the burdens of your deceptions
Hoping for someone to expose you
That you may end this double life

Think not that your false charm
Will not betray you
Pretty packages are eventually unwrapped
To disclose the waste within

YET

It is not okay
How you hurt me
Months later
The pain is still intense

Time heals all wounds
I wish that it would do it faster
Time also makes me more angry
As I understand what you did to me

You took the innocence
That only dating after remarriage can reconstitute
Knowing that I had it
You trampled on it

Decades of arid sexuality
Now led to unrestrained passion
Teenage like lust emerged
The portion of me that had died with the marriage

You Dirty Rotten Filthy Pig

You knew that I was vulnerable
A 45 year old virgin with two grown children
You ignored what your perverse ways
Would do to me

In the end
You proved yourself to be scum
And me
The debris that you kicked to the wayside

Reclamation

If I have given you the power to hurt me
I reclaim it
And let you go

If I have given you permission to control me
I release my heart
And take back my sovereignty

When I confront you
I am filled with longing
Lose my resolve

Solutions are never as simple
As the situations
Which created them

SHATTERED

I should be glad
That you are not here
To pull my mind apart

It should be relief
That I feel
To not have you in my heart

I should be thankful
Not to have to
Put up with your rages
Or your behavior
Which is outrageous

Your drunkenness
Disorients me
Spins me around
Confuses me

Is it you?
Is it me?
What do you want?
Pain has shattered
Torn apart my heart

DIAPERS

Poopy pants
It is time for you to clean
Your own crap
Not me

How dare you give me
Your underwear
With a sheepish grin
Expecting me to clean your shit

I am not your mother
Hire an ass wiper for yourself
Lovers do not wipe excrement
Unless there is a sexual game involved

GONE

No longer will I know
Where you are
Or what you are doing

No longer will I remain
Connected to you
24/7

I have said good bye
And am moving on

Already you feel it
Sense it in my remove

You do not feel me
With you anymore

And with good reason
Already I am gone

Allyson Moore

FOOL

It was a lie
It was all a lie
The whole thing is a lie
Your life is a lie

How could I have deluded myself
Into believing you?
You are a master of deception
And I the fool who bought into it

RED THONG

There was a time
When I thought
That I
Couldn't live without you

There was a time
When I planned
My activities
Around your schedule

There was a time
When I specifically dressed to please you
To arouse you
To get your dick hard

There was a time
When my hair style mattered
When I dressed in short skirts
Plunging neck lines

I wore a red thong
With black lace and a slit in it
To show off another "best part" of me
Those times are done
Eat your heart out

New Chapter

I find that as I end other chapters in my life
That I wish to continue
The one that I had been writing with you
I hadn't realized that I had been missing you

The day has come
When the chaos of the storms
That we created
Has passed

Although a part of me wants to write a new story
    with you
I am still tied to the fear
That held me in bondage to you for a time
I can never go back

LAST DANCE

My last dance is not going to be with you
You are not going to be the last man with whom
I slow dance
Before I retire to my seat

You are not going to be the last man to hold me
In the last dance of my life
Your arms not the last
To guide my steps

You are not going to be the last man
To press his body into mine
So that my memory of my last dance
Is with you

FREE

I feel like I have been raped by you
Because I am denied my voice
I am told that nice
Irish Catholic girls
Do not say
Anything

I feel like I have been strangled by you
That your hands are around my throat
I am told that nice
Irish Catholic girls
Who want to go to heaven
Keep their mouths shut

I feel like my identity was taken away from me
When I struggled against the injustice
I was told that nice
Irish Catholic girls
Who do cry out
Are hurting Holy Mother Church

Not anymore
I am done
I no longer subscribe to rules
Which I did not create
Which protect the powerful
Harm the innocent

Nice
Irish Catholic girls
Who are not prepared to yell
To scream out the truths of injustice
Will never be heard
It is time to no longer be

A nice Irish Catholic girl

I ASKED

One unselfish evening
Was all I asked for
When your self absorption
Would not preclude me
From the conversation

An evening of true companionship
When you would leave your ego
Parked at the door
When the recital of your accomplishments
Was silenced

A few hours
Of genuine interest
When a question for me
Was not the platform for you
Talking about yourself

I wanted to know
If you had any real interest in my kids
If you were capable
Of asking about my life
Without patronizing condescension

You Dirty Rotten Filthy Pig

I didn't think it was much to ask for
From a man who professed to love me
Yet even that
Seemingly
You could not deliver

LEAVING

This is what he does
He leaves
His power takes him into places
That I do not see

This is what I do
I stay
My power takes me into places
That he does not care to see

He goes out to battle
The proverbial warrior
Trying to satisfy his boredom
Seeking an eternal adrenaline rush

I create a fortress of love
The true nurturing mother
Providing sanctuary for hearts in need of healing
A castle of delights for my children

Always he must run away
Taking a part of my heart with him when he goes
Slowly, imperceptivity
I have become inured to his travels

PAST TIME

There was a time when I didn't think that I could
Live without you

There was a time when I didn't think that I could
Walk past the phone without hearing your voice

There was a time when I didn't think that I could
Watch the sunrise without thinking of the beauty
Of the love that we once shared

There was a time when I didn't think that I could
Get dressed without wondering
If you thought that my outfit would make me look sexy

Although those memories of you are burned into
    my heart
I find that I now can

Allyson Moore

HOLE

Faced with the overwhelming issue
Of moving on
I find
That I can't

I don't want to take the risk
Of being wounded again
I fear that I am becoming bitter
Lost

I swore that I wouldn't become like this
But after years of loving you
Like I did
I am

It is now impossible for me
To be willing to take the risk of
Handing over my life again
Into another relationship

FLAVOR OF THE WEEK

It was all a game
And I
The unwitting token
Used by an experienced player

The innocent divorced virgin
Awoken from her marital slumber
Another conquest
Added to the missed opportunities of your youth

Awakened
I sought new levels of sexuality
Became the temptress
Had fun playing the whore

Was it my wicked intelligence
Garbed in the corporate uniform
That drove you to erotic fantasies and
Thus into my arms?

Naive
I was stunned that you became bored so quickly
Your manic need to spill your seed
Likely a sex addiction

STOP

Stop
I beg you

Stop
Why are you hurting me?

Stop
Don't do this

Stop
Can't you see what you are doing to me?

Stop
Don't you care?

Stop
Please

PREFERABLY ALONE

I say no to you
And to what you mean
I don't want you in my heart
You don't fit into my scheme

You should be dead to me
Gone from in my heart
Stay away from me you madman
I prefer to be alone in the dark

Allyson Moore

THOUGHTS WHILE WRITING A REPORT

I find myself missing you
During off moments like this
When I shouldn't

I should have let go of you
A long time ago
But haven't

You have invaded my thoughts
Once again
Undermined my peace

Distracted me
Forced me off track
Left me wondering

As to where you are
What you are doing
Why you aren't with me

I retreat into that place of hurt
Where I am reminded of your lies and infidelities
Thankful that I had the strength to leave you

Nouveau Trash

A good education
Means nothing to you
Do something useful
Don't be such an old fool

Taking you out of the jungle
May not make you tame
Some animals are controllable
Some beasts will not train

You have generations of old money
But act nouveau riche
Dress it up in beauteous splendor
Trash always stinks

Allyson Moore

TASTEFUL MEMORIES

Delicate hues
Attend your skin tone
Golden light
Molasses colored caverns

I sought those secret places
Where I could nibble
Suck
Where I could pull your skin with my lips

Your heaving orgasms
My wet panties
The wastebasket filled with condoms
Are gone now

For me
The memory lingers
For you
I suspect that I am gone with the trash

TARGET

Constant criticism
Wrecked terrible damage
It's as though you
Were hurtling knives
Slowly killing me

I withstood the pain
Uncomplaining
Hoping
That it would stop
But it didn't

You tore at my self esteem
Attacked my self confidence
Tried to convince me that you
Could not trust me
So I began to distrust myself

In time I stopped listening
To my inner guidance
Began to wonder if I was stupid
Ugly
Unloved

I isolated myself
To stop the barrage of pain
Withdrew
Found solace in places
Removed from you

Though I pled with you
In subtle ways
The torture never stopped
You drew strength from my helplessness
As your abuse increased

CAUTERIZE

January
Led to February
Led to March
Led to April
And so on

I can now recount
The days
The months
Without the sharp edges of pain
That consumed my being

Time does not heal
All wounds
Often we need
To cauterize them
To stop the bleeding

Allyson Moore

Bondage

Stop stalking me
In my heart
I turn my brain on
And you are there

It is not fair
That you are with me
At all times
Why don't you get the hell out?

This is nothing but torture
Pure
Unmitigated
Unasked for

I feel helpless to do anything about it
Leave me the fuck alone
Before the depths of my pain
Kill me

BOBBIT

OMG
Where did you get those silk boxers?
I didn't give them to you

HOW COULD YOU?
You were with another woman
How dare you wear them with me!

I WANT TO THROW UP
You are such a pig
Didn't you think that I would notice?

IT'S TIME FOR A BOBBIT
Get the hell away from me
Before I am tempted

No Choice

This is very painful for me
I wish that you felt about me
The way that I feel about you

I feel so cut off from you
Like I am connected only when you choose
I don't like the lack of choice on my part

I could end it
Part of me
Wants to

Yet I am unable to do so
Emotional dependency
Has weakened me

SIGNIFICANT OTHER

I look up to see
If you are standing in my doorway
I glance to see
If you are sending emails
Then conjecture who you are writing to

I know that you have said
That there are no significant others in your life
However I do not feel
As if I am the significant person in your life
Either

Allyson Moore

SO THERE!

Societal rules dictate
That I be nice to you
Even after all of your abuse

You are a filthy piece of trash
A man whore
Every bit a promiscuous slut

Don't tell me that I cannot fight back
It is precisely that attitude
That got me here in the first place

I am no longer going to keep my mouth shut
You are going to be held accountable
Consider this your notice

THE CASSOCK

The cassock does not change you
Slip your arms into the sleeves
You are not transformed

Arrogant
Unyielding
Narcissistic

You still invade
Pervade my thoughts
Consume my energy

Take off your chasuble
You are a weak man
Driven by big passions

Protected by those
Who are worse
Than you

Unbridled
Not tamed
By an authority

To which you claim
To submit to
But don't

BELONGING

Your life is one of pretend
You are here
But you are not

You are there
But that is false

You say that you belong
But nothing could be further
From the truth

You do not belong to me
You belong to no one

Allyson Moore

MOVING ON

As though beaten with a stick
I knew that I had to move on

I was reluctant
To begin the journey
To leave the past behind

I was afraid that I would
Never scale
Those heights again

I still am

YOU PIG

You pig
You said that you would call
Its 12:15
You said that you would call at 9

You pig
I am sitting here
Getting increasingly frantic

You pig
I am waiting
Don't you care?

You pig
My emotions matter
Once again you have shattered them

Allyson Moore

SUNLIGHT

Random patterns of sunlight
Filtering through the trees
Onto my window pane
Fascinate me

I watch the edges of the sunlight
Move and grow
Change shape
Change glow

Light descending into a
Darkened forest
Reminds me
That there is hope
But I know that there is none

It's Discouraging to Know

It's discouraging to know
That you wont give our love a try

I sought to climb out of the desert
And reach unto the sky

You told me that you loved me
But that was all a lie
You had a set of mistresses
They were
Bourbon, gin and rye

I sought to find the heavens
And bring it back to earth
Find fire
Love
And passion
And enjoy
The wonder of rebirth

TOXIC

Capricious qualities
Do not excuse you
From taking responsibility
For your actions

Captivating though they be
Intriguing as they are
You are a dangerous
Quantity

Solitary
Independent
Secretive
A chameleon

I really don't know who you are
While I sought to discern that over time
I am now done
You are not worth the trouble or time

Good bye

MANNERS

You didn't hold the car door
Open for me
That was a sign
That you were moving on

You neglected to pull the chair
Out for me
That was a sign
Of your growing disrespect

You no longer held the office door
Open for me
That was a sign
That you were closing the door on our life together

For a while
I missed these subtle signs
Now I read them just fine
They cannot be ignored

Allyson Moore

PINING

It is sickening to watch my behavior
I am like a teenage girl getting over
Her first broken heart

I am weepy
Telling my story of how you hurt me
To anyone who will listen

I check the phone too often
Hoping that you will call me
Yet dreading that you might

HUMP

We moved into an
Uncomfortable friendship
Like dogs who
Sniff each others asses
Then hump

No foreplay
No interchange
No emotion
I felt so much regret

In taking me like that
You asserted your dominance
Sex done
There was nothing else

MYTH

We are prolonging the myth
Of the Warrior
Hunter

We are creating
The captivity
For ourselves

By portraying ourselves as
Trophies
Prizes

In pushing the males to chase
We create
Demi-gods

Who think that it is
Their right to rule
To subrogate

It is time to release ourselves
From the tyranny
That we have falsely created

DECEPTION

In the light I saw
Who you were
In the darkness
You were disguised

Sleight of hand
Magical games
Nuance
Misdirection

These were all tools
Used to deceive me
Now that you are unmasked
Be gone!

ALONE

I fear that I will not be whole without you
The whole that I have come to know
By being with you

It is a struggle that I do not wish to face
The pain of being alone
Having to find my own place

The darkness scares me
I do not know how to fill it up
If you leave me I am forced to fill it with myself

I do not know who I am
Who am I?
How do I fill this space?

Come back to me
So that I can find my false self
Go away so I can find the true one

RENT

You pig
You gambled away our first month's rent
On a horse race

I was panicked
You were pissed
At my reaction

Three years of living together
Before we got married
You never did such a thing

On that golden fall day
I didn't marry Michael
I wed Jekyll and Hyde

WITHDRAW

I control my own heart
Although I had determined
To spend my emotions on you
I can withdraw them

I have the strength to give my love
Where it will be cherished
I will not die
I will continue to move on

Although I had thought that
My destiny was entwined with yours
You have given me enough doubts to be concerned
I will cut it off

I still love you
But tomorrow I will seek
Someone who won't hurt me
Like you do

WEDDING CAKE

I weighed 112 pounds on our wedding day
My wedding dress hanging on my thin frame
A tea length, sheer, Jacquard

Ceremony
Reception
Cake

The ritual completed
My new husband yelled at me
For having a second bite

Humiliated
I left the reception
Before anyone could see my tears

Allyson Moore

IT IS HARD TO LET GO

It is hard to watch
Someone that you love
Turn to someone else
Even though you know
That they weren't meant for you

It is hard to listen
To someone that you love
Share lover's secrets
Even though your heart
Still yearns for them

It is hard to be rational
When the one you love is gone
Your emotions get in the way
You want to throw your arms around them
And have the loneliness go away

NO JUSTICE

One wife
One girlfriend
A dozen other women who left messages
$1000 worth of calls to live telephone sex lines

I was the mother who satisfied all of your needs
Your girlfriend was the whore who satisfied all of
    your fantasies
The personal ad hookups satisfied your boredom
The sex calls, your masturbation needs

It took me a long time to understand how
A man with a crooked dick
Could entice so many women to have sex with him
Your performance in court
Proving that there is no justice for women

CONNECTION

I look up hoping to see you standing there
But knowing that it would be an illusion
In my weaker moments
I wish to call you forth

Knowing the damage
That it will create
I will not do so

You are the shadow
In the mists of my life
The image that I see in the background
The augury of desolation

Within my heart
Your presence causes destruction
My life becomes a wasteland

In the absence of finding the union
That I sought
I must move on
To find it with someone else

It is time for you to leave
My heart and my thoughts
I now disconnect my ties to you

FARTED

I can't believe
That you just did that
You farted
Loud and clear
Silent and deadly
Now you are looking around
As though pretending
That someone else
Is the perpetrator

Allyson Moore

LANDFILL

The restraining order in place
For your attempted strangulation of me
We entered our home from which the police
Had removed you several hours prior

It felt like a tomb
As though the life had
Been sucked out of it
A shocking amount of trash on the floor however

As I stood there hand in hand
With our pre-school aged daughters
I was filled with horror as I realized
That all of the debris littering the floor was
    pornography

Secure from seeing the proof of their fathers
    depravity
I discovered that he had stuffed
All of the bathroom heating vents
With it as well

Although I kept my composure
I lost the contents of my stomach as we left
My once beautiful home
Now a landfill for a sex addict

ADORATION

Fascinating temple
I peeked inside
Desired to enter

I climbed the altar
Worshipped it on my knees

As the monster was lifted
I paid homage
Filled with adoration
I was consumed

BIRTHDAY

It was my birthday
Coinciding remarkably
With a major sporting event

We were young kids
Not very well suited to one another
With limited financial means

When I balked
At the purchase of a TV
As MY supposed gift

You stormed out of the apartment
Ignored my birthday
Broke my heart

HARM

When you harm me
You harm others
When you hurt me
You hurt all who love me

We do not exist in
An isolated world
All of our actions have a cause
And an effect upon others

My daughters suffered
Because you caused me to suffer
Warning them that men cannot be trusted
As you callously strutted your newest hookups
    through my life

My girlfriends watched in helplessness
Unable to intervene
Rallying to my side
Trying to put me back together again

I am still raw from the rigors of dealing with you
It angers me that I was in love with a man-whore
I wish that your dick would
Catch a disease and fall off

CRAP

Waste baskets are available for a reason
You useless excuse for a man
Snot rags go in them
Not in the bed

There are garbage bags
For a reason
You worthless slob
Trash goes in them

Garbage cans are out
For a reason
You lazy pig
The trash in the bags goes in them

PHONE

I'll talk with you later
How I hate those words
In the beginning I thought
That they meant
That you would call me in the evening
Fool that I was
I sat by the phone every night
Waiting for your call

It was shocking to me
Over time
How cavalier you were
With your words
They had no meaning
While I took them at face value
You manipulated them
To suit you own needs

BLAME

At some level
I have continued to blame myself for our break up
I was too fat
My belly wasn't flat
I wasn't pretty enough
I was too much of a bitch

I was none of those things
I made sacrifices that I didn't know that I was even
     making
I kept trying to please you
When I should have quit
I was oblivious to the truth
I didn't deserve how you treated me

All the while
You told me that nothing that I did was good enough
I wasn't thin enough
My belly had too much roundness
I wasn't beautiful
I deserved to be treated like I was

You Dirty Rotten Filthy Pig

It had nothing to do with me
I took the blame unnecessarily
I was too thin
My roundness made me look like a woman
I was breathtaking
You were just a dick

LESSONS

Though you sought to discredit them
The wounds were real
The emotional bleeding intense

In brushing off my emotions
You were seeking
To abrogate your responsibility for them

You had no interest in me
It was only your own pleasure
That you sought

When I complicated our lives
With my feelings
You discarded me

DROVE

The tragedy of our relationship
Is that as you
Climbed out of the bottle
I walked out of your life

In the years that it
Took to drive me away
You killed the spirit inside me
You drove us apart

Allyson Moore

The Weekend

The long awaited romantic weekend
Filled with endless possibilities for wanton sex
In a hidden beachfront cove

We lost ourselves in one another
Our cries mingling
With those of the seagulls

As balmy breezes
Soothed the heat
That our bodies created

Our parting on Sunday bittersweet
Confirming that I would keep my heart for you
Then not hearing from you for six months

You are scum

I TOOK IT AWAY

Eat your heart out
You dirty rotten filthy pig
You could have had me with you
If you had not been such a prig

I loved you to distraction
Was willing to sacrifice myself for you
Would have gone to the ends of the earth
Been in love with you until our lives were through

I demand you look at me
Knowing that it is hard
As I leave to seek another life
While yours will always be an empty jar

I have regrets that much I can say
I gave my heart to you
Then regretfully
Took it away

ALONE AGAIN

Do I move on?
Or sit still?
Do I wait?
Or continue to hope?

I have cried
I have grieved
I have counted the minutes
I have counted the stars

I sit alone again tonight
Frantic
Lonely
I am not at peace

THE FEMALE ZOHAN

We had been separated a month
You called me in desperate need
The bookies were going to hurt you
Unless you paid your debt immediately

I gave you my rent money
Expecting it back within days
You avoided my calls
I could not track you down

Now facing eviction
I left one final message
Give me back my money within the hour
Or I would begin to make calls

Beginning with your girlfriend
Then your boss
I would divulge
The real reason for our breakup

An hour passed
I placed my call
Your hideous screaming notwithstanding
I was paid before the two hour mark

The female Zohan has left the room

DEPARTURE

It was my birthday
A day I looked forward to cherishing
With my husband and best friend

Scattered papers on the table
I picked them up
As I grabbed a cup of coffee

His handwriting jumped out at me
"She is a sweet woman but I am in love with you"
These words written as I slept on the eve of my
    important day

In horror I stood there betrayed
Knowing that I had just lost
The two who mattered most to me

Having no money I kept the knowledge of their
    deception to myself
Until making a dramatic exit from our marriage
At a restaurant on our First Anniversary

CAST OFF

I am angry at the way
You have betrayed my love
I freely gave it to you
Only to have you throw it back in my face

Cast off worn out sweater I was
Discarded in a heap
For the cats to knead their paws in
I deserved better than this

Politics

What could you have ever seen in her?
An older woman but not a cougar
30 to my 20
Saggy breasts to my firm

A convenient lover from the campaign trail
Were you so stupid as to believe that I would not
    find out?
Young though we both were
You had enemies, while I had protectors

When your affair came to light
I became unwilling to live that life
Abandoning politics
Walking away

PRECIPICE

You did not seek
Because you did not know
What to find

You chomped on swill
Not knowing
How you poisoned yourself

In your desperate acts
Of self hatred
You drove yourself

Into the wall
And me
Off the precipice

Allyson Moore

HOOK DICK

All those years of drinking
The cirrhosis
Phlebitis
The other complications of which I was not aware

Did not prepare me
For what popped out of your pants
At that critical moment
A fish hook shaped erection

Thankfully
I did not gasp
Having had some reasonable sense of composure
Yet not knowing what I could do with it

Could I
Touch it?
Lick it?
Mount it?

Eventually I married it
Dooming myself to a largely sexless life
My husband dying
Before the release of Viagra

GOOD BYE

That kiss was good bye
Although you may
Not have known it

My tongue tasted
The etchings of
Your lips

I stared into your eyes
Imprinting upon my mind
Their radiant depths

I searched your face
For every indentation
Scar
Age spots
Every wrinkle

Knowing that I may not
Feast upon it again
But wishing to retain
The memory

STENCH

Pigs come in many varieties
Little ones
Big ones
Those that roll in the mud
Those who walk on a leash
Those who are 6 feet tall walking on 2 legs

Do you smell that odor?
The stench of your foulness
Has permeated
Every aspect of my life

Your filth dirties me
Your depravities seep into me
Your rot fills me
I am nauseated

There is a dense stank
It is the smell of my shame

INSTANT

In an instant
I found my voice
The extremes of your behavior
Driving me to speak out to others
After a lifetime of struggles
I understood that I was free to make a choice

Whatever the outcome may be
I have started down a path
Whose end
I cannot see
But which I am compelled to follow
In order to recover from you

CLOSING

In the end
It was inevitable
One of us had to leave the pig sty
It was me

Although you had attempted
To bring it into my household
I rejected
Your scheme

Unwilling to join in your depravity
To live in that filth
I gradually gathered my strength
Then proudly left

The quizzical look
Upon your face startling me
That you were so detached
From your actions

I closed the barnyard door